The ALEFBET ILLUMINATED

Written and Illustrated by Alex J. Rajic

cenozoic press

Mazel Tov! To the Aaronson Family

Alex Rajic 12-05-2010

The Alefbet Illuminated

ISBN: 978-0-615-38180-0
Library of Congress Control Number: 2010913151
Copyright © 2010 by Alex J. Rajic
All rights reserved. Published by Cenozoic Press, Orange CA.

Cover design and interior illustrations copyrighted © 2010 by Alex J. Rajic.

No part of this book may be reproduced in part or in whole, by any means, mechanical or electronic, without written premission from the author. For information regarding reproduction for educational purposes, please contact the publisher at info@cenozoicpress.com.

Printed in Canada
First Printing
Cenozoic Press
354 Via La Canada Unit 7
Orange CA 92869, USA

www.thealefbetilluminated.com
www.cenozoicpress.com
www.alexrajic.com

*Dedicated to the memory of my grandparents,
Enid and Don Dunkleman*

ACKNOWLEDGEMENTS

There are many people without whom making this book would not have been possible. First, I would like to thank my mother, Fern Rajic, for always supporting me and my dreams. I thank my father, Michael Rajic, for helping me simultaneously keep my feet on the ground and my head in the clouds as well as introducing me to the wonders of digital design and art programs. For always taking the time to listen and look every time I finished *half* a painting, I thank my brothers, Aaron, Jeremy, and Benjamin. My grandparents, Enid and Don Dunkleman, deserve my deepest gratitude for inspiring me to never settle for anything less than amazing. Although they never got to see the book completed, I remember them every time I paint a stroke or write a single word. I would also like to thank Rachel Dunkleman for her infinite enthusiasm along this journey. I also owe my gratitude to Eran Itzkovitch, my good friend, for bringing an insider's perspective on the Hebrew language. It took me two years to muster the courage to write the poems in this book and I thank Jake Kilroy for guiding me towards the end result. Finally, I would like to thank Jan Osborn for rekindling the fire through her amazing philosophy on literacy.

INTRODUCTION

Like any Jewish child, I first learned to read and write Hebrew in the third grade as preparation to become a Bar Mitzvah. Although I was initially resistant to the idea of attending Hebrew school, my youthful resistance transformed into an ever-growing wonder and passion for an extraordinary heritage. Learning Hebrew has come to be one of the most satisfying and important things I did as a child. Though I never learned to speak Hebrew fluently, I wanted to continue the tradition of Jewish book-making, and inspire Hebrew literacy in both children and adults. I found that learning Hebrew, even at the most basic level, is possibly one of the most essential and unifying acts of becoming a member of the Jewish community.

The pages that follow combine paintings, letters and words in hopes that the reader comes to share this same passion for Jewish heritage and the larger human heritage of learning and creativity through language. Even as an artist, I believe a picture may be worth a thousand words, but a single word can be worth a thousand ideas. With that in mind, I hope this illustrated book helps bring the reader closer to the Hebrew language and the world of ideas that it embodies.

ALEF

Alef is for aryeh.

An airy aryeh
Aidly resides in his arid abode—
imagining, wondering,
anticipating the auspicious eve.

BET

Bet is for barboor.

Baby barbooreem bask and bob beneath a beautiful plumed body and broad, billowing wings in the balmy, brilliant lake.

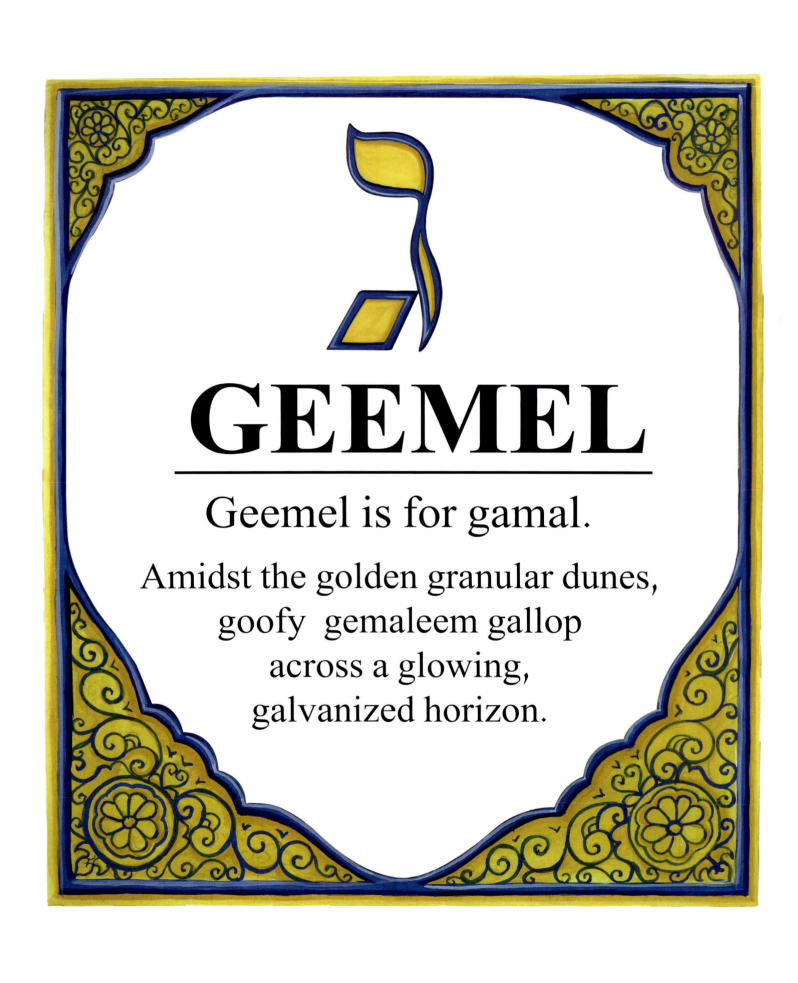

DALET

Dalet is for dov.

A delightful dov,
Denizen of the wintry desert,
dangles her digits-
dawdling, deliberating,
daring to dive from her den into the frigid waters below.

HEH

Heh is for heepopotam.

Hefty.
Huge.
Herculean.

Heepopotamot huddle and hide in an aqueous haven of harmonious hues.

VAV

Vav is for velotseeraptor.

A vicious and veracious velotseeraptor vehemently veers across a vast, vapid valley, cloaked in a variegated vest of feathers.

ZAYEEN

Zayeen is for zeekeet.

Confused or clumsily irresolute? The bizarre zeekeet cruises zealously under a dynamic disguise.

KHET

Khet is for kheepoosheet.

Acantankerous kheepoosheet of ochre complexion crawls up a crusted tree, concealing its complexity.

TET

Tet is for tavas.

The tantalizing tavas totes his ostentatious, towering tail of twinkling turquoise and teal.

YOD

Yod is for yanshoof.

A judicious yanshoof quietly rests under a large yellow moon. The yowls of another echo as it glides through the gleaming nocturnal sky.

KAF

Kaf is for kelev mayeem.

With the cadence of the cool waves, the curious kelev mayeem clasps clams and urchins with her crafty claws.

LAMED

Lamed is for leevyatan.

Luminous.
Lofty.
Their longitude looming,
Leevyetaneem float through a liquid landscape with astonishing levity.

MEM

Mem is for makaw.

Marvelous mottled makayeem meander in the misty, muggy jungle with melodious mirth and intrigue.

NOON

Noon is for nakhash.

The nefarious nakhash writhes and winds nimbly around nodules of knotted wood.

SAMEKH

Samekh is for soos.

Soaring across the grassy green savanna, beneath a tranquil sky, a swift, sinuous soos springs and sprints.

AYEEN
Ayeen is for 'atslan.

Ascending the airy boughs,
hanging upside down,
an amiable 'atslan embraces her
delicate young.

PEH

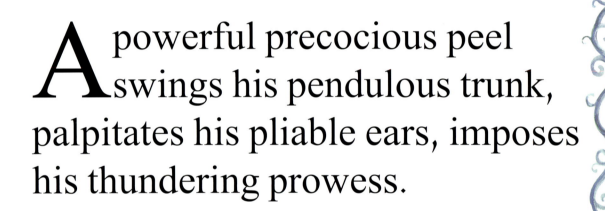

Peh is for peel.

A powerful precocious peel swings his pendulous trunk, palpitates his pliable ears, imposes his thundering prowess.

TSADEE

Tsadee is for tsfarde'a'.

Sticky mitts affixed to plants, waxy glistening tsfarde'eem mingle in the moist nocturnal forest.

KOOF

Koof is for kof.

Carefully perched on a tree, a quirky, inquisitive kof gawks quixotically.

RESH

Resh is for rakhel.

Ruffled, rambunctious ruminants.

Rekheleem rhythmically race as a rampart across dry, rosy earth.

SHEEN

Sheen is for shoo'al.

Secretively, a sly shoo'al scours the icy arctic scene, shrouded in shimmering snow, seeking a semblance of shelter.

TAV

Tav is for taneen.

The tenacious taneen
trudges near teeming waters,
thrashing his terrible tail,
baring his terrible teeth,
retracting his terrible toes.

The ALEFBET

ה	ד	ג	ב	א
HEH	DALET	GEEMEL	BET	ALEF
י	ט	ח	ז	ו
YOD	TET	KHET	ZAYEEN	VAV
ס	נ	מ	ל	כ
SAMEKH	NOON	MEM	LAMED	KAF
ר	ק	צ	פ	ע
RESH	KOOF	TZADEE	PEH	AYEEN
			ת	ש
			TAV	SHEEN

GLOSSARY

Aryeh/arayot: lion(s)
Barboor/barbooreem: swan(s)
Gamal/gemaleem: camel(s)
Dov/dobeem: bear(s)
Heepopotam/heepopotamot: hippopotam|us(-i)
Velotseeraptor/velotseeraptoreem: velociraptor(s)
Zeekeet/zeekeeyot: chameleon(s)
Kheepoosheet/kheepoosheeyot: beetle(s)
Tavas/tavaseem: peacock(s)
Yanshoof/yanshoofeem: owl(s)
Kelev mayeem/ kalbey mayeem: otter(s)
Leevyatan/leevyetaneem: whale(s)
Makaw/makayeem: macaw(s)
Nakhash/nekhasheem: snake(s)
Soos/sooseem: horse(s)
'Atslan/'atslaneem: sloth(s)
Peel/peeleem: elephant(s)
Tsfarde'a'/tsfarde''eem: frog(s)
Kof/kofeem: monkey(s)
Rakhel/rekheleem: sheep/ewe
Shoo'al/shoo'aleem: fox(es)
Taneen/taneeneem: alligator(s); crocodile(s)

האלף-בית
מאויר

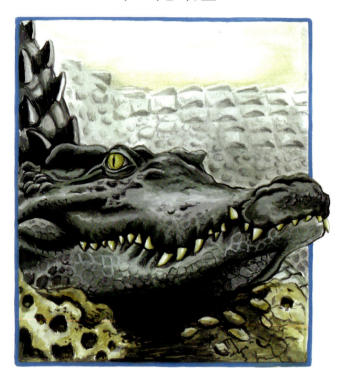

אלכס ראג'יק

cenozoic press